Nature Inspired

MIXED-MEDIA TECHNIQUES for
Gathering, Sketching, Painting, Journaling, and Assemblage

QUARRY

Nature Inspired

MIXED-MEDIA TECHNIQUES for
Gathering, Sketching, Painting, Journaling, and Assemblage

Tracie Lyn Huskamp

BEVERLY MASSACHUSETTS

QUARRY BOOKS

First published in the United States of America by
Quarry Books, a member of
Quayside Publishing Group
100 Cummings Center
Suite 406-L
Beverly, Massachusetts 01915-6101
Telephone: (978) 282-9590
Fax: (978) 283-2742
www.quarrybooks.com

Library of Congress Cataloging-in-Publication Data
Huskamp, Tracie Lyn.
    Nature inspired : mixed-media techniques for gathering, sketching, painting,
    journaling, and assemblage / Tracie Lyn Huskamp.
        p. cm.
    ISBN-13: 978-1-59253-536-1
    ISBN-10: 1-59253-536-4
1. Nature craft. 2. Handicraft. 3. Photography. I. Title.
    TT157.H787 2009
    745.5—dc22

                                                                  2009006057
                                                                  CIP

ISBN-13: 978-1-59253-536-1
ISBN-10: 1-59253-536-4

10 9 8 7 6 5 4 3 2 1

Cover Design: Nancy Bradham
Book Layout: Sandra Salamony
Photography: Lightstream

Printed in China

*This book is dedicated to everyone who
has ever been inspired by the magnificent beauty of nature
and longed to capture a little of its incredible splendor.*

NATURE RAMBLES

SPRING IN THE WOOD

Contents

Introduction

NATURE INSPIRES THE IMAGINATION and captures the heart with its wonders. It is part of our everyday lives, surrounding us in even the most urban landscape. We only have to step outside the front door to be greeted with bursts of colorful foliage, hear bird songs on the breeze, run our fingers through the grass, or smell the sweet fragrance of flowers. Sometimes, the unexpected happens, and we're surprised by nature experiences that are not so common—spying a small rabbit resting under a shrub, for example, or a mother duck wading in the water followed by a procession of ducklings. These experiences help us feel connected to this vast world and draw our spirit closer to its beauty.

Longing to hold on to these heartfelt moments, we cling to small findings, hoping to sustain the memories by bringing them inside. However, we quickly find that the flower withers; the leaf curls and turns brittle. So, we gather sturdier treasures—sticks, seashells, pinecones, or rocks—only to have them collect like clutter, and then discover that we don't know how or even where to display them. Is there a way to hold onto our delicate finds or arrange our collections to capture the precious moments of communing with nature in a way that keeps those experiences fresh?

Often, we observe nature with nothing to help us record our personal encounter. How do we document those particulars? Perhaps we're fortunate to have a camera with us at the precise moment that nature reveals itself. We are even lucky enough to snap a few pictures. Yet, all too often, we find out later that our reaction was too slow, the photo is blurry, or the print is too dark. Can we salvage these mishaps and turn them into cherished mementos? What if we have several photographs of a number of subjects, but not one perfect shot containing all the desired images? Is it possible to create a single likeness from these not-so-perfect pieces?

The answer to each of these questions is a resounding *yes*! We can use several art methods to accomplish this task, including painting, journaling, collage, and assemblage. By combining elements both natural and manmade, we can create lovely nature sentiments that chronicle our experiences and bring the outdoors in.

If you've tried any of these art methods before and found them difficult or unsuccessful, you might feel uncertain about trying them again. But, by applying a few simple techniques, with some helpful hints and tips, you'll find it easy to achieve beautiful commemorative works that preserve lasting memories, decorate the home, and provide years of enjoyment.

Finding Inspiration in Nature

FROM ONE MOMENT TO THE NEXT, nature is ever-changing. This is especially true if you have watched a sunset. Twilight has always been my favorite time of day. As the sun begins to set and shadows dance across the floor in a slow waltz, I often find myself drawn outside. On warmer days, I sit on my front porch completely mesmerized by the parade of colors marching across the horizon. The sky, with its vast array of tints and tones, seems to blend and shift in mere seconds. Although short-lived, this daily performance always starts with fiery oranges, vibrant turquoises, and brilliant pinks that give way to soft, muted colors of dusty purple, peachy pink, and pale aqua. The spectacular show always ends with a curtain call of midnight blue.

Like the sunset, other changes in nature also seem to happen in the blink of an eye: an open flower closing at dusk, a resting bird that flies away, a sunny blue sky turning to gray. In your quest to use natural subjects in art, you'll find it helpful to have access to some basic equipment, such as a camera, small notepad, writing instrument, temporary plant press, and varying sizes of plastic bags. These will help you record those fleeting moments and gather mementos to use later, when working in the studio.

Capturing Nature with Photography

ONE OF THE BEST WAYS to preserve a nature moment is with a photograph. These days, you can find a wide range of cameras that yield varying results, depending on the make and model. You don't necessarily need to own an expensive piece of equipment to capture a good nature image. Remembering to zoom in as close to the subject as possible provides the largest range of options for transforming that image into art.

Image Details

When shooting a photograph, ideally, the image should contain as many fine details as possible—the more details that are visible, the more accurate the depiction of the subject. The best times to take outdoor photographs are on overcast days and at dawn or dusk. If the day is bright and sunny, it also helps to move the subject into the shade. Shade conditions provide a more even distribution of light, illuminating all areas of the subject and revealing finer details. Unfortunately, a photographer does not always have the luxury of moving the subject into the shade or choosing the time of day or weather conditions. If you are unable to place the subject into the shade, try moving around it, to find a camera angle that best highlights the subject's shape and texture.

Image Clarity

To capture a clear photo, it's important to hold the camera as still and as steady as possible. Mounting the camera to a tripod is the best way to keep the equipment stationary. If you can't attach the camera to a tripod, rest the camera on a stable surface. Many cameras now offer image-stabilization technology; think about investing in one if you're planning to use the camera for nature photography.

A moving subject is much harder to capture. In these instances, working with a camera that offers a stop-motion setting is best. If your camera doesn't have a stop-motion function, try shooting the photo when the subject is at rest.

TECHNIQUE

Avoiding Hot Spots

Hot spots are extremely bright, almost white, areas in the image caused by the light from a camera flash bouncing off a reflective surface. When light is more concentrated in one area than in any other part of the scene, you can lose details. Although some cameras have settings to help control the use of the flash (check your camera manual for the correct settings), many point-and-shoot models don't have these options. If your camera does not offer flash control, you can use a number of methods to control it without changing a camera setting.

- **Step back from the subject to reduce the severity of the flash.** Although you would normally stand close to the subject to fill the frame of the viewfinder, this can cause the effects of the flash to be brighter.

- **Use the zoom function.** A close image of the subject can be captured without sacrificing detail due to lighting or distance.

- **Control the light coming from the camera by diffusing it.** Place a semi-opaque material, such as tissue paper or vellum, over the flash. Be sure to use a white material—another hue will alter the color of the light cast by the flash.

- **Redirect the flash onto a different surface, rather than directly at the main subject.** When taking a photo, you normally center the subject in the viewfinder. To redirect the flash to reduce hot spots, place the subject slightly off center. Keep in mind that the color of the surface from which you bounce the light can alter the colorcast of the photograph.

- **Add more overall light to the scene.** Or position yourself to take maximum advantage of available natural or ambient light.

Collecting Botanicals

I NEED ONLY TAKE A SHORT WALK around my neighborhood, yard, or garden to gain inspiration from the beautiful trees and plants I see. I love gathering botanicals to use in my art. Including a piece of nature in an arrangement of manmade materials gives the piece a delicate, soft, and authentic quality.

Gathering Flowers and Leaves

Gathering objects for your artwork is not hard to do. Bring along a pair of small pruning shears, gardening gloves, and a white or light-colored basket. The light color makes it easier to spot bugs crawling out of a botanical. Also consider wearing long pants, a light-colored, long-sleeved shirt, socks, good shoes, and a hat, especially if you're collecting in a wooded area.

- The best time to gather botanicals is around midday, when petals and leaves are the least damp and completely open.

- The look of the plant when dried will be the same as it was when picked, so select specimens with the best appearance. Flowers in the early stages of blooming are the most vibrant.

- After gathering a plant, give it a gentle shake to remove bugs.

- If the plants or leaves you want are already on the ground, choose those that have had the least amount of exposure to moisture. Avoid taking specimens from the bottom of a pile or that have been lying in a puddle.

- Time is of the essence. Once a plant has been cut from its stem, it is essential to start the preservation process as soon as possible, by carefully arranging the flower or leaf between two pieces of blank newsprint and drying it in a plant press. The pressing process removes the moisture and prevents mold. (See the *Gathering Journal,* page 58.)

- Fall is an excellent time to collect colored leaves. However, some leaves change color as they dry. Red leaves retain most of their original color, with some fading; green leaves fade dramatically or turn brown; yellow leaves can also turn brown or fade to a soft orange; and orange leaves deepen toward a brownish hue.

- Be sure to ask permission if picking botanicals in a location other than your own yard. It is illegal to collect leaves, flowers, and branches in parks or to trespass on private property without authorization. When collecting, remember that the natural specimens gathered, along with the surrounding environment, are an important part of our ecosystem, so be careful not to upset or destroy the delicate balance that nature has created by picking more specimens than necessary.

Gathering Branches

Limbs and branches can add great dimension and height to an artwork.

- Be sure to completely strip your collected branches of all foliage; leaves left on the branches will turn brown, curl, and eventually crumble as the limb dries. If you do choose to leave the foliage on the branch while it is drying, be especially gentle when handling the branch—even the tiniest movements can cause withered leaves to fall and crumble.

- Give newly collected branches a gentle shake to remove bugs.

- Allow branches to thoroughly dry.

- Small twigs attached to the branches can be brittle and tend to snap off easily, so be extremely careful when working with them.

- Prune the limb before you use it, and avoid trying to tear or remove a piece with your hands. You risk losing the bark or breaking the branch in an undesirable location. Cutting the branch with shears ensures that it looks the way you intended.

Gathering Birds' Nests

ONCE THE LEAVES HAVE FALLEN from the trees, remnants of seasons past are easily visible. A bird's nest is one such treasure that might be nestled among the now-bare limbs. Occasionally, you might find a nest blown from a tree by a storm. These delicate objects must be treated with great care. The assortment of manmade materials our feathered friends gather and weave into the nest walls—Christmas tinsel, cassette-tape ribbon, dryer lint, housing insulation—is interesting to see. I was once given a nest from a friend, who made small funnels from the pages of catalogs and magazines and tucked them into trees to encourage birds to build in the yard.

Cleaning Seashells

Cleaning the shells before using them in art or decorating is a must, because seashells can retain a strong odor. I like to leave remnants of barnacles and algae on my shells, because I think it gives them a more natural look, so I scrub my seashells in very hot, soapy water and lay them out to dry in the sunshine. However, to completely rid shells from the natural buildup:

1. Soak them in a solution of equal parts water and bleach. Bleach can be harmful to the skin, so be sure to wear protective gear, such as gloves and goggles.

2. Soaking time depends on the individual shell and the amount of buildup. Leave the shells in the mixture until all the algae is gone.

3. Stubborn barnacles might need to be removed with a dental pick or toothbrush.

4. After removing the shells from the bleach water, rinse them with fresh water and allow them to dry thoroughly.

5. Give the clean shells a nice sheen by rubbing them lightly with baby oil.

Cleaning Live Seashells

Occasionally, you might find a seashell with animal tissue still inside. Before collecting a live shell, check with local authorities regarding policies on gathering live specimens. In some areas, this is against the law. Before cleaning the shell, it's important to remove the animal tissue. There are several ways to do this. You can bury the shell in the dirt and allow the bugs and other microorganisms from the soil to eat the animal remains, or you can place the shell in a waterproof bag and freeze it for several days. You can even microwave the shell, if you don't mind the smell. Another method is to boil the seashell in water.

1. Allow the water to boil for several minutes before submerging the shell to ensure that the water is at its highest temperature. Leave the shell in the boiling water for approximately 2 to 3 minutes.

2. Use tongs to remove the shell from the hot water, and wear gloves before handling it.

3. Carefully remove the remaining tissue, and rinse the shell with cold water.

4. Follow the cleaning instructions to clean your now-empty seashell.

Cleaning Starfish, Seahorses, and Sand Dollars

The methods for cleaning starfish, seahorses, and sand dollars are a little different from the methods for cleaning seashells.

1. Soak starfish or seahorses in 70-percent isopropyl alcohol for approximately 12 hours, and then dry them in the sun.

2. To keep the starfish from curling during the drying process, place small weights on the legs.

3. Place sand dollars in fresh water almost immediately after gathering, to preserve their white color.

4. The soaking water will quickly turn brown and odorous, so be sure to change it often.

5. Continue soaking the sand dollar in fresh water until the water remains clear, then soak it in a solution of equal parts bleach and water. Be sure to soak it for no longer than 10 minutes, to prevent the sand dollar from crumbling.

6. Rinse the sand dollar with fresh water and dry it in the sun.

Alternative Nature Remembrances

PRESERVED NATURE SPECIMENS can be beautiful components in your art or home décor. However, there are alternative methods for bringing the splendor of the outdoors inside. Leaf rubbing, plant printing, and flower pounding are simple, fun activities that don't require a cleaning and preservation process. The results can be added to a journal, used as a background for artwork, to create a special card, or can be framed as a reminder of a particular location or trip.

Leaf Rubbings

Leaf rubbings are an inexpensive, quick, and colorful way to create a nature remembrance. Using plain copy paper and crayons, you can capture the leaf contours and interior details of live botanicals.

Experiment with art pastel sticks, charcoal sticks, and even a sharpened pencil held sideways.

Crayon Prints

1. Start by collecting specimens of all different shapes and sizes.

2. Be sure to use fresh leaves for this process; dried leaves are brittle and can crumble under the pressure of the crayon on the paper.

3. Towel-dry the leaves to remove surface moisture and dirt that might rub off onto the paper.

4. Position the leaves faceup, on a smooth, flat surface.

5. Place a piece of white tracing paper or copy paper over the leaf. A lightweight, pliable paper reveals the most details from the rubbing and yields the best results.

STEP 5

6. Select a favorite crayon or water-soluble art crayon with the paper wrapper peeled off. Holding the leaf and paper steady, press the crayon down and gently rub it over the paper-covered leaf. An image of the leaf will begin to appear on the paper.

7. Continue rubbing the paper until the entire leaf shape is captured on the page.

8. For variety, rub several leaves using varying colors on the same page. You can also vary the colors in a single leaf.

tip

Pastel and charcoal sticks are messy and give only an impression of the leaf silhouette without capturing many of the fine details. Light pressure yields the best results; too much pressure results in a color blob. The sticks can be used on both lightweight paper and card stock.

Nature Prints

Nature printing is an age-old practice used by both artists and scientists to record the natural world around them. Here are three methods for creating a nature print. The first two capture leaf or plant silhouettes; the third requires applying color directly to the natural object.

TECHNIQUE

Watercolor Silhouettes

This is a fast and easy method for printing a plant or leaf silhouette.

1. Start by selecting a piece of light-colored, absorbent paper, such as watercolor paper or even some handmade papers.

2. Because only the outer edge will be seen, choose a fresh plant or a leave with an interesting shape.

3. Carefully towel-dry the plant to remove surface moisture and dirt, and then lay it on the paper.

4. Tuck the specimen between two sheets of plain newsprint paper and place it under a heavy book. Press for 30 minutes to flatten it as much as possible.

5. Using water, a paintbrush, and watercolors, create a mixture of water and paint (known as a wash) on the palette.

6. Holding the plant or leaf steady on the page, begin applying a light wash of more paint than water to the paper, making sure to paint past the edges of the botanical.

7. Avoid applying too much paint at once—you don't want the colors to bleed under the edges of the plant or leaf. Sweeping strokes across the entire leaf works best.

8. Allow the leaf to dry thoroughly, then apply another wash to intensify the color.

9. Continue the drying and painting process until a satisfactory amount of color is showing on the page.

tip

Avoid using more than two different paint colors in one area. When multiple colors are mixed, they can look muddy.

NaturePrint Paper Silhouettes

The second method for creating a silhouette is through the use of a sun-sensitive paper, such as NaturePrint Paper. This method requires no special processing, inks, chemicals, paints, presses, or photo equipment. Queen Anne's lace is a beautiful flower to use with this paper because the intricate stems and floral bursts can be easily captured.

1. Choose dried or relatively flat botanicals and insects for this method.

2. Use the frame that comes with the paper to hold the paper and objects in position, and then place them in the sun.

3. Once in the sun, the silhouette will begin to appear on the paper; it will be completely printed in approximately 2 to 3 minutes.

4. To stop the processing of light onto the paper, soak the paper in water for 1 minute and hang to dry.

tips

Be sure to have the water bath prepared before starting.

Take care not to get the kit's paper frame wet. This is easy to do when fumbling to get the paper into the water.

THE SUN PRINTS IT!

NATUREPRINT® PAPER
SUN PRINTING KIT

TEACHER DESIGNED KIT CONTAINS:
80 Sun-Sensitive Sheets
Exclusively Ours: PRESS • PRINT • FRAME • HOLDER
6 Transparencies — Many Images on each including
8 Greeting Messages
18 Wildlife Drawings
Snowflakes, Hearts, Shells
Cars, Motorcycle, Space Shuttle

PLUS! Surprise Plastic Pattern!

SINCE 1977

Produces Beautiful Prints from Natural or Manmade Objects

NATUREPRINT® PAPER undergoes a chemical change when exposed to sunlight. Images appear in minutes and are permanent.

NATUREPRINT® PAPER P.O. BOX 314 MORAGA, CALIFORNIA 94556

Direct Color Prints

The third method for making nature prints is to record an image by applying color directly to the desired specimen.

1. Select a piece of light-colored absorbent paper, such as watercolor paper or even some handmade papers.

2. Carefully towel-dry the fresh plant or leaf to remove surface moisture and dirt.

3. Have several pieces of plain newsprint paper ready for practice prints or for blotting a freshly inked botanical. Be sure to keep a supply of absorbent papers, newsprint paper, and cover paper handy during the printing process.

4. Select a favorite color of block printing ink to use for printmaking. Squeeze a few drops onto the paint palette.

5. Dip a cosmetic sponge into the color, blot off the excess paint, then dab the paint onto the specimen. Continue until the entire botanical is coated with a thin layer of paint.

6. Place the painted botanical facedown on the newsprint paper, cover it with a piece of copy paper, and press down firmly. To avoid smearing the print, be careful not to move the painted botanical once it is on the paper.

7. Lift the painted specimen off the page with tweezers to avoid smearing the paint.

8. Practice the printing process on newsprint paper until you determine the correct amount of paint to apply to the leaf and pressure required to make a good print. When you feel comfortable with the practice pieces, try the process on good paper.

tips

Another way to apply color to the botanical specimen is to roll a brayer through the block printing ink, and then roll the colored brayer over the botanical.

Acrylic paints are a reasonable substitute for the block printing ink. However, when using acrylics, it's much more difficult to achieve an even coat of paint over the entire specimen. To ensure that the surface is completely covered, you might need to overlap areas. Another downside to using acrylics is their lack of a pasty consistency, which is needed to create multiple printings. This makes it difficult to do test prints before using the technique on good paper.

Flower Pounding

Flower pounding is the art of transferring pigment from a floral specimen onto paper or fabric. Start by selecting a surface that's sturdy enough to withstand banging with a tool—an old cutting board works well. Although a hammer can be used for pounding, a rubber mallet is preferred because of its wide contact surface. A rubber mallet is also lighter and easier to maneuver and will not make dents in the paper, which a typical steel hammer can.

Flower Pounding on Paper

Flower pounding should be done on absorbent papers, such as watercolor paper, tea bags, or coffee filters. Ideally, you want to achieve a muted copy of the flower with distinct color areas and crisp outer edges. If the paper is too slick, only random spots of color might appear after the pounding. Pounding on paper that is too absorbent leaves more plant residue on the page, as well as pigment that is very faded with less crisp edges. If you're using watercolor paper, choose a 90-lb. (190-gsm) weight, rather than 140-lb. (300-gsm) or 300-lb. (640-gsm), because it is absorbent but not too absorbent.

1. Select flowers with thin, brightly colored petals. If a flower has multiple petal layers, separate the layers or use individual petals, one at a time.

2. Cut the stems from the flowers, just beneath the flower head.

3. Place the flowers facedown on the paper and cover them with a piece of plastic wrap to keep the flower in place. Press-and-seal plastic wrap works the best, but plain plastic wrap can also be used if it's secured to the page with a piece of white artist tape.

4. Cover the now-secure flowers with another sheet of paper and hit the paper with the mallet. Move the mallet over all areas of the flower and strike each area more than once.

5. When finished pounding, carefully remove the plastic wrap. You should have a crisp silhouette of the flower with distinct solid areas of color on the page.

When using the press-and-seal plastic wrap, another lighter print can be made by securing the plastic onto a fresh sheet of absorbent paper and pounding the areas holding flower residue.

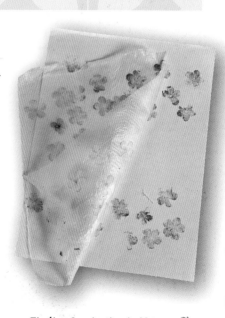

Flower Pounding on Fabric

Fabric is also a great absorbent material for flower pounding. Natural fibers, such as cotton, silk, and linen, can easily absorb the flower pigment. To create flower-pounded fabrics, use the same techniques used for flower pounding paper. After pounding, set the image before washing the fabric, to keep the design from disappearing.

A simple way to set the image is to soak the fabric for approximately 2 or 3 minutes in a solution of ¼ cup (230 ml) salt to 5 cups (1.2 L) warm water. Be sure to stir the mixture, so the salt dissolves and doesn't collect at the bottom of the bowl. The salt bath removes plant residue that might remain after the pounding and sets the fabric. Wash the fabric in cold water using the gentle cycle.

The flower images will fade significantly and can change colors after the fabric dries. To keep the image from rapidly fading, store your art out of the sunlight. Over time, however, all colors will eventually fade or change colors, some more than others. Yellows fade quickly, greens can fade to a yellowish color, and pinks can appear purple. Blues are the most fade-resistant.

Finding Inspiration in Nature 31

Rendering Nature

WHEN I WAS OFFERED the chance to work from the comfort of my home studio, I jumped at the opportunity. In a matter of weeks, I saw changes in my daily routine. Instead of rushing out for a fast-food lunch, I spent the noon hour soaking up the outdoors and wandering through my neighborhood, photographing nature and gathering bits of inspiration to bring inside. Slowly, I built a collection of treasures and photographs, and the subject of nature became a recurring theme in my work.

Although I had taken several drawing classes in college, I found the process tedious and actually preferred painting. With paints, I felt free to be as detailed or abstract as I desired, and I could express my ideas with color. I wanted to paint the nature images I was capturing with my camera. But I wanted to paint them without having to first spend a lot of time drawing the subjects. So, I began to explore other methods of rendering an illustration from a photograph.

The techniques described in this chapter are the result of my explorations. By following these simple methods, you can transform a favorite photo into a finished painting, without having to rely on drawing skills.

MY heart is awed within me when I think
Of the great miracle that still goes on
In silence round me—the perpetual wor...
Of Thy creation, finished, yet renewed
Forever. Written on Thy works I read
The lesson of Thy own eternity.

Sketching from a Photograph

In this technique, you'll use a favorite nature photograph to create a sketch onto fabric, paper, or other substrate. The sketch will serve as the base for your painting.

Collecting the Images

To begin, you will first need a suitable photo. You might have several photographs or have jotted down notes on more than one interesting subject encountered on nature outings. Choose a subject that captures your imagination and calls out to be turned into a painting. Select photos of the desired subject or subjects that provide a clear silhouette image with large interior details, such as facial features, legs and tail, stem, petals, or leaves. The background is not important, unless you plan to incorporate it into the painting. If this is the case, try to simplify the background to allow the main subject to clearly stand out.

You don't have to limit the number of elements you use or base your piece solely on what was captured in a single photograph. You can combine elements from several photographs or even reference materials (if you can't find a photo) to create a single work of art.

Preparing and Printing the Photograph

Once you've chosen a photo (or photos), you might find that it needs some enhancing before you can use it as a reference. Your chosen photo might be dark or slightly blurry. Perhaps your subject is too small for the details to be seen. If you are using multiple subjects, you might need to crop and resize the subjects, so they match in scale. You want to make sure a clear shape and the larger details of the subject can be identified.

Image-editing software, such as Adobe Photoshop, can help correct a less-than-perfect photograph. If you don't have access to editing software, you can take your photo to a local copy center or print shop, where trained staff members can help you with specific needs. If all attempts to fix a photo fail, look for another photo or check out copyright-free nature images and choose one that speaks to you. You can also consult a favorite book distributor or ask friends or relatives if they have photographs that might be suitable for your project.

tip

You can gauge the correct lightness of the image by laying another piece of copy paper over the original copy
image. Clear outlines of the image and major details
should be visible when the two sheets of paper are held
up to the light.

ORIGINAL IMAGE

AFTER MANIPULATION

1. Start by scanning the photo into the computer.
   Remember to set the scanner resolution at 300 dpi
   (dots per inch) if enlarging the image. If you want
   your final image to be the same size as the scanned
   photo, or smaller, a resolution of 150 dpi is fine.

2. Using photo manipulation software, crop in on the
   desired subject, if necessary, and resize the cropped
   area to the appropriate length and height for the
   project. Next, correct any errors in color, lighting,
   contrast, and sharpness. The results can vary,
   depending on the capabilities of the program used.

3. Once the photo has been sized and enhanced, lighten
   the image an additional 30 percent. Lightening the
   image makes the subject details more distinguish-
   able, especially when the subject is a similar color
   throughout the body, or when the subject blends into
   the background of the photo. The percentage is
   approximate and might need to be adjusted more or
   less, so that light details are not lost, but dark areas
   of the subject are illuminated.

4. Finally, print the image onto a sheet of typing or copy
   paper. This image is your reference for the sketch.

Making the Sketch

The prospect of drawing can be daunting, especially if you have never had any training or feel you have no talent. Or perhaps you think it's too time consuming. But there is an easy way to draw a subject without the need for art classes—tracing. By practicing this simple method, you can acquire a repertoire of drawing skills through familiarity with an object. Eventually, you might even feel confident enough to sketch the subject freehand.

There are two methods for tracing the sketch from the photocopy. The first uses a light box, the second uses graphite paper. The method you use is determined by the material you choose for your painting.

Choosing Your Substrate

Before choosing your painting surface, or substrate, consider how you will use it in your final artwork. You can paint the image, or you can choose to simply color the sketch with pencils or markers. You might even want to cut the subject from the substrate and use it in a mixed-media piece. With your end use in mind, choose the substrate that works for you.

If you want to paint the image with acrylic paints, keep in mind that you might need to make some adjustments to the chosen material. Some substrates need prep work before they can be painted on—raw canvas, for example, needs a coat of gesso. Others might require additional coats of paint to ensure that the surface is completely covered. The material can also affect drying times between coats of paint. How well the paint covers and blends will also be determined by your substrate. You might have to adjust the ratio of paint to water.

Fabric is an ideal choice, because it is flexible, fairly strong, and more resistant to moisture than paper, which tends to disintegrate when it gets wet. It also lends itself to a variety of applications, including sewing, appliqué, collage, and assemblage. Paper, watercolor paper, vellum, glass, canvas, wood, dried gourd, ceramic greenware, and acrylic can also be used as substrates. Be sure the material you choose can withstand water and paint without crumbling.

If you are working with fabric, consider using cotton muslin. Cotton is non-stretchy, with a matte luster and has excellent absorption capabilities. Cotton muslin is typically unbleached or white and, because it has no pattern or printed design, it provides a smooth, even surface for painting. Use muslin with a 200 thread count. The weave of a muslin fabric with a thread count higher than 200 is too dense to see through to the photocopy on the light box (see Tracing an Image Using a Light Box, page 37). The weave of a muslin fabric with a thread count lower than 200 becomes more noticeable, because the spaces between the thread strands are large. The loose weave also makes it difficult to spread the paint evenly across the surface. (You can find thread-count information on the cardboard inserts of fabric bolts.)

It's not necessary to wash the fabric before using it. Most fabrics have had sizing medium applied to them before they are shipped to retailers. The sizing helps the fabric retain its shape and resist dirt. Normally, fabrics should be washed before working with them, to remove the sizing, preshrink the material, and preset colors that might bleed. However, washing the fabric causes the tiny fibers that make up the thread strands to stand up, rather than remain flat, which makes it difficult to spread acrylic paint across the surface.

Materials

- transparent or semitransparent substrate
- photocopy of subject
- mechanical pencil with 0.5 lead
- clean white eraser
- artist tape
- light box

Tracing an Image Using a Light Box

A light box is a frame that projects light through a translucent surface (usually plastic or glass). These are relatively inexpensive and can be found at art and craft stores. If you don't have access to a light box, you can use a brightly lit window. When working with a light box, you must use a substrate made of a transparent or semi-transparent material, such as muslin, paper, or vellum, so that the photocopy image can be seen through it.

1. Place the photocopied image on the light box or window and secure it in place with artist tape.

2. Position your substrate over the image and secure it on all sides with artist tape.

3. Using a fine-point mechanical pencil, carefully trace the image onto the substrate, recording as much detail as possible. (A 0.5 lead gives a crisp line and leaves less graphite on the fabric. A heavier graphite line is much harder to erase.)

4. When you've finished tracing, add details to the drawing. Leave one side of the tape attached to the substrate, while lifting it away from the light box to check that all the details have been captured. The secured side will help you place the substrate back in place to finish the drawing.

Artist tape is a good choice for securing items and is easy to remove when you are finished. You can find artist tape in art stores or in the art section of hobby and craft stores.

Materials

- nontransparent substrate
- photocopy of subject
- red ballpoint pen
- clean white eraser (optional)
- fine sandpaper (optional)
- graphite paper
- artist tape

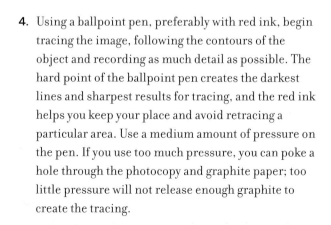

Tracing an Image Using Graphite Tracing Paper

This method uses graphite paper and a ballpoint pen to create the sketch onto an opaque substrate, such as canvas, wood, dense fabric, or watercolor paper. To transfer an image onto one of these materials, the substrate is placed under the photocopy print, with the graphite paper sandwiched between the two.

1. Secure the substrate to the work surface with artist tape.

2. Carefully position a piece of graphite tracing paper, dark side down, over the substrate. Be careful not to handle or lean on the tracing paper too much, because the layer of graphite on the transfer side rubs off very easily.

3. Lay the photocopy image on top of the tracing paper, being sure to place the image exactly where you want it to appear on the substrate, and secure it on all sides. Do not move the substrate, graphite paper, and photocopy once you begin tracing—this can cause unwanted smudges and shifted lines.

4. Using a ballpoint pen, preferably with red ink, begin tracing the image, following the contours of the object and recording as much detail as possible. The hard point of the ballpoint pen creates the darkest lines and sharpest results for tracing, and the red ink helps you keep your place and avoid retracing a particular area. Use a medium amount of pressure on the pen. If you use too much pressure, you can poke a hole through the photocopy and graphite paper; too little pressure will not release enough graphite to create the tracing.

5. When finished tracing, check the drawing by reviewing the red lines drawn and making sure important details are not forgotten, then carefully remove the photocopy and tracing paper. If you leave an unwanted smudge on the substrate, use a clean eraser or piece of fine sandpaper to remove the graphite. The tracing paper can be reused several times, until the graphite is gone.

Filling in the Details

You now have a contour drawing of your desired image on a substrate. Before you continue to the painting or coloring process, add more detail to the illustration. If the subject is a wildlife image, be sure that facial features, such as the eyes, nose, and mouth, are included in the drawing. Pay particular attention to their exact placement and size on the face, and don't forget to capture the white spot seen in the pupil of the eye. When looking at pictures, people tend to focus more on the face than on the rest of the body, so being accurate with these elements is critical. If the subject is a flower, focus on the details represented in the center of the blossom, such as the stamens or seeds and the larger veins seen throughout a leaf or plant. Specific details help the viewer quickly recognize the subject portrayed in the artwork. If your photocopy is not clear enough to discern the fine details, consult wildlife or botanical reference books for help.

Filling in the Details

Finishing the Illustration

Although the detailed contour drawing still needs an application of color, you don't necessarily have to paint it. It is perfectly fine to simply color the illustration and the surrounding background to create a finished piece. If you plan to paint the illustration, use the techniques in the rest of this chapter.

In this piece, antique lace, sheer fabrics, and a swan painted on muslin fabric are stitched to a dyed piece of unprimed canvas. The piece is decorated with miscellaneous ephemera such as vintage papers and buttons.

Painting Nature on Muslin

The idea of painting nature subjects on muslin arose when I was looking for something to do on a snowy New Year's Day. I had been admiring some large nature tapestries in a favorite fiber magazine and had the urge to create my own lush nature artworks. Although I didn't weave, I wanted to re-create the vibrant colors I had seen in these fabrics, so I turned to paint and white muslin fabric. I had painted on canvas and watercolor paper before but wanted to try working with a more versatile substrate, one I could use with both paper and fabric in my collages. I came across a large bin of craft paints that had long been forgotten. I pulled out every bottle and began experimenting.

Using Acrylic Paints

Acrylic paint is an excellent medium for capturing natural subjects. It dries quickly, mistakes can easily be covered up with additional coats of paint, and it comes in a myriad of colors, which almost eliminates the need for mixing paints to obtain a particular shade. Acrylic paints can vary dramatically in price from brand to brand—the cost of artists' fluid acrylics, for example, can be three to five times higher than the price of craft

paints. Some lines offer huge color selections; others provide rich, deeply saturated colors and are more fade-resistant. Consider the overall look you wish to achieve and investigate several brands of paint to find the right one for your project.

Although it might seem difficult, painting is a matter of training the eye to see the range of colors in a subject, noting the subtle shifts from one color to the next, and then translating that information to your illustration. Consider taking a photocopy of your nature subject with you to the craft store. Hold the photo up to the display of paints and gather the colors you see in the image.

Some of my favorite paint colors, the ones I use most often when painting nature subjects, are white, black, light gray, burnt umber, raw umber, beige/cream, pale purple, olive green, medium foliage green, light foliage green, sky blue, navy blue, French blue, Prussian blue, bright yellow, medium golden yellow, bright orange, and burnt orange.

tip

When choosing paintbrushes, look for those specifically made for acrylic painting. You want the brushes to retain their original shape, with a relatively sharp point, after dunking them in water. Avoid brushes that are floppy and tend to bend easily while painting.

Materials

- unwashed white muslin fabric (200 thread count)
- acrylic paints
- double-sided fusible webbing for fabric (optional)
- heavy gel medium (optional)
- brush for applying gel medium
- #1, #3, and #5 round paintbrushes
- 1" (2.5 cm) flat paintbrush
- mechanical pencil with 0.5 lead
- clean white eraser
- paint palette
- water cup
- rag for cleaning brushes
- scissors

1. Start by drawing the photocopied nature subject onto the substrate. If you are using muslin or another semitransparent substrate, follow the instructions for Tracing an Image Using a Light Box on page 37. Once the outline and pertinent details have been drawn onto the muslin, you are ready to begin painting.

2. Load your palette with the appropriate colors of acrylic paint for the project. Have a clean rag handy for cleaning the brush between color changes. Remember to keep the water relatively clear by changing it when it becomes muddy; dirty water can alter the color of the paint.

This piece features a thin piece of embroidered fabric, and vintage lace is stitched to an old ledger page. The meadowlark is painted on muslin fabric, embellished, and extracted from the original background using techniques referenced on page 45.

3. Before you begin applying paint to the substrate, break your subject down into 4 to 6 large color areas. Start by laying down those large color blocks and leaving the detail work for later. Don't ignore areas—it's important to work the entire piece, so that same level of detail is consistent throughout the painting. This also gives wet areas time to dry.

4. When there is a shift from one hue to the next, blend the colors together. Avoid leaving hard lines between color shifts, which can make the subject appear choppy and unconvincing. Be sure to allow adequate drying time after painting each color. Overworking wet areas with a brush will cause the colors to become muddy; it can also spread color into areas in which that color isn't wanted.

KEEPING PAINTS MOIST

Acrylic paints on the palette can dry out quickly. To keep paints pliable, try one of the following options:

- Add acrylic retarding agent to the paints.

- Use a white polystyrene foam plate as a palette and cover it with plastic wrap if you're away from the project for more than 5 minutes. Press-and-seal plastic wrap works well.

- Use a wet paint palette to create a moist atmosphere. You can buy a wet palette kit, which comes with a hard plastic tray, sealing lid, tray sponge, and acrylic palette paper, at an art store, or you can make your own by placing 4 or 5 damp paper towels under a piece of palette paper in the bottom of a shallow plastic container with a lid.

5. Don't be concerned with capturing every detail perfectly. Focus on major details first. For animals, concentrate on the face, especially the eyes, nose, and mouth, and the distinct markings that make a species instantly recognizable. For flowers, concentrate on the blossom, the center stamen, and the shadowing where petals overlap or attach to the center. For plants, concentrate on the major veins of the leaves. Adding a few details in the right places can make a huge difference to the look of the painting. Adding several tick marks that represent feathers, for example, can give the illusion that a bird has more feathers than those actually depicted.

6. Although painting dark areas can be daunting—if you paint something too dark, how do you fix it? Mistakes are easy to cover with acrylic paints, so don't be afraid to use dark paints. Dark areas are the deep shadows that help a flat illustration look three-dimensional and help make the image appear more realistic. For shadowy areas, consider using a very dark brown color, such as raw umber, as a substitute for black. Dark brown radiates a warm glow, whereas black tends to have a colder feel. Build up shadowy areas with thin layers of paint and water, called a wash, to achieve the correct level of depth.

7. Take occasional breaks from the painting. Looking at a piece with fresh eyes helps you spot areas that need more work. Also, stepping back at least a foot or two from the project can help you better see the piece as a whole and helps identify trouble spots.

As bottled fluid acrylic paints get older, they lose their fluidity and tend to become thick and gummy. Instead of throwing the paints away, thin them with fluid additives, available from the fine-art-supplies section of art and craft stores. You can also add fabric medium to acrylic paints to enhance their workability on cloth. In some cases, the medium allows the painted fabric to be washed. When buying additives and mediums, try to choose the same brand as the paint brand and follow the instructions on the bottle.

Life must be what we make of it.

Embellishing the Subject

Once the image is painted and dry, you can take some artistic license and add embellishments to the subject. Embellishments can include bits of old lace adhered to a bird's wing or colored thread stitched around the inside edge of a flower's petals, leaves, and stem. Buttons, pearls, sequins, beads, vintage rhinestone jewelry, rubber stamp designs, decorative rub-ons, and pieces of illustrations or words from a book or magazine can add fun detail. Another idea is to experiment with decorative

fabric interfacing and other bits of sheer material with a design. Something unexpected can add just the right touch to an area that needs some sparkle.

Embellishments can be adhered with heavy gel medium, stitching, or double-sided fusible webbing. Be careful when ironing on the fusible webbing; cover your work with several sheets of parchment paper, and never iron the painted side of the artwork—always use the iron on the back of the painting.

Pulling It All Together

ART SCHOOL PROFESSORS may insist on creating a background along with the main subject in an artwork—the proper, formal way to create a work of art. As a mixed-media artist, one can take liberties. You might want to cut your subjects from the material or paper and adhere them to a completely different decorated background.

Once your sketch is painted, it is time to put the finishing touches on the final artwork. Whether you have cut the painted nature subject from the background or painted the entire substrate with a nature scene, be sure that the subject blends into the final background, so no one element looks out of place.

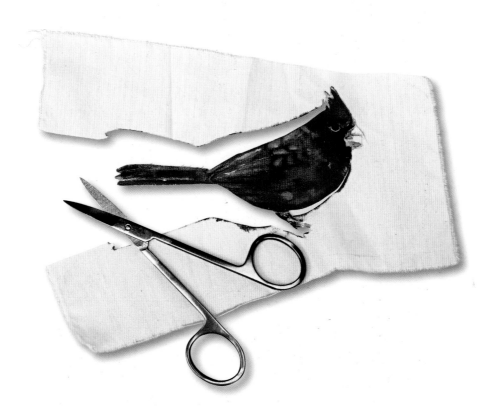

Extracting the Subject from the Background

Once the contour sketch is painted, it is perfectly fine to color the surrounding background to create a finished piece. However, consider removing the painted subject from its original background and attaching it to another material. If you plan to cut the subject from the background, be sure to eliminate all traces of the original background—even the tiniest remnants can hinder the realism of the final art. Also, be sure to finish the cut edges of the painting. If the extracted piece will be seen in the forefront of the final artwork, tint the edges

the same color as the face of the piece. If you want the extracted piece to blend into the new background, tint the edges the same color as the background. To create a convincing single surface from multiple elements, adhere the pieces onto a surface that is as smooth as possible. The thinner the piece you are adhering, the more important this is. If the surface of the piece is smooth but is rough on the backside, shave away as many rough spots as possible. Avoid gaps, bumps, and bubbles between the substrate and the attached elements.

Three-Dimensional Effects

If the substrate can be easily cut with scissors or a craft knife, consider making pieces of the painted subject three-dimensional. Create a 3-D effect by tacking down only parts of the subject and letting the remaining parts, such as the wings of a bird or the petals of a flower, lift away from the background.

If you are using muslin, which is thin and doesn't stand up on its own, you'll need to back it with a stiff material. Felt or felt sandwiched between the painted muslin subject and another fabric works well. Use double-sided fusible webbing to attach the layers.

When your subject is sturdy enough to stand up by itself, decide which parts you want to keep free and sew the rest to the background. For example, sew the butterfly body to the background but leave the wings unattached, so they lift away from the body. Or sew only the upper portion of a bird's wing to the background, so the end feathers are three-dimensional.

Shadowing

Creating shadows is an important technique for achieving a seamless integration of elements. Shadows give two-dimensional works a three-dimensional appearance. Although it's common to see shadows in paintings, we often forget to include shadows in mixed-media works. Shadows give the illusion of depth and help draw the viewer into the picture. Even if shadowing does not exist naturally, when adding an element to the artwork, consider what type of shadowing it should have. Is the element close to the background or far away from it? Does a shadow make sense or help make the picture convincing? If a shadow is needed, is it thin, dark, and close to the subject element—which gives the illusion that the subject is close to its surroundings—or is the shadow soft, light, and large, to suggest that the element stands away from the surrounding spaces?

If your piece isn't looking as cohesive as you'd like, consider adding an overlay of sheer fabric or tulle. Applying thin layers of clear varnish or sealer can also help unify the work, as can clear encaustic wax. Use caution when applying wax. Elements in the art can react or change after the wax is applied; the paper or fabric can look darker, for example, or appear wet. The wax can also cause images and writing on the back of an element to show through.

Distressing Techniques for Backgrounds

IN NATURE PHOTOGRAPHS, the subject can often be surrounded by a muddle of hard-to-distinguish elements. Branches, leaves, grasses, flowers, trees, and plants can seem to blend together in a complicated and intricate pattern that can distract from the main subject. But it's not necessary to include all the details in a scene to capture the essence of a subject's surroundings. You can create the illusion of nature by using distressing techniques that resemble those interesting, complex backgrounds.

tip

Cover your work surface with plastic and have paper towels handy for cleanups and for blotting excess water or product. Before you begin using distressing techniques that involve water, be sure to set up an area in which your substrate can dry. Stains can drip onto other surfaces, so be sure to lay down plastic.

TECHNIQUE

Dyeing with Instant Tea

Tea dyeing is an age-old process that gives fabric and paper a worn, vintage look. The traditional method of tea-dyeing involves bringing a pot of water to a boil, adding a number of tea bags to the hot water, and soaking the fabric in the mixture until the desired effect is achieved. A quicker, easier way to tea-dye fabric, paper, and other substrates is to use instant tea.

1. Pour a tablespoon (15 ml) of instant tea granules into a bowl.

2. To create a wash, fill a small, fine-mist spray bottle with tap water and spritz the granules until a teaspoon (3 ml) of dark liquid appears.

3. Using a 1" (2.5 cm) flat paintbrush, distribute both the wet granules and dark liquid over the background areas of the substrate.

4. Spritz water directly onto the fabric to dilute the stain and cause it to spread and create interesting color variations. The stain can take longer to completely soak into other substrates, such as paper. Give the tea adequate time to seep into the fibers before spritzing, to garner the most color.

tip

Some flavored instant tea granules have been colored and can give the liquid hints of this same coloring when the stain dries on the substrate. Peach-flavored tea, for example, leaves a slight orange tint, raspberry tea is reddish. It is perfectly fine to use flavored teas—just be aware of their effects on your background.

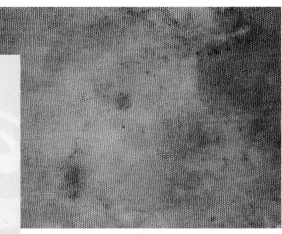

Walnut Ink Crystals and Sprays

Walnut ink can also give fabrics and paper a vintage look. The ink is available in crystal and spray forms. Tsukineko Walnut Inks, which come in roughly eight colors, were used for the examples.

Using Walnut Ink Crystals

Walnut ink crystals can be used in much the same way as instant tea.

1. Pour a teaspoon (3 ml) of crystals into a bowl.

2. Fill a small, fine-mist spray bottle with tap water and spritz the crystals until ¼ teaspoon of colored liquid appears.

3. Using a 1" (2.5 cm) flat paintbrush, distribute both the wet crystals and the colored liquid over the background area of the substrate.

4. Spritz water directly onto the fabric, or use a paintbrush and clean water, to dilute the stain and cause it to spread and create interesting color variations.

tip

Have a bowl of clean water handy when using walnut inks and sprays. They are color intense and yield the best results when diluted with a paintbrush and clean water after they're applied to the substrate.

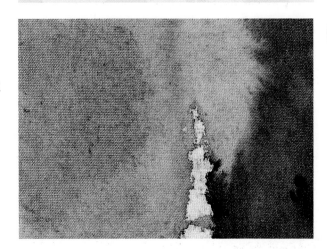

Using Walnut Ink Sprays

Walnut ink sprays are walnut ink crystals that have been premixed with water and made available in spray bottles. Sprays create intense areas of color that fan out into lighter, scattered color, interspersed with drippy dots of color. Be sure to cover your painted subject before spraying the background areas. If ink drips onto your subject, wash it with clean water until the original paint color is restored.

1. Spray the ink onto the fabric or paper.

2. Using a 1" (2.5 cm) flat paintbrush, apply clean water onto the fabric or paper to dilute the stain and cause it to spread and create interesting color variations.

3. Continue spraying ink onto the fabric until the desired intensity is achieved.

tip

Always do a test spray on a paper towel to gauge the color intensity and workability of the spray pump before using it on the substrate.

TECHNIQUE

Dye-Na-Flow and Bleach

Dye-Na-Flow is a liquid opaque fabric paint manu-
factured by Jacquard. Straight bleach applied to fabric
painted with Dye-Na-Flow strips most of the color away
and creates a halo effect in the area where the bleach is
most concentrated.

1. Use a dry brush to paint the fabric with Dye-Na-Flow.

2. To control the spreading of the bleach, wait until the
   Dye-Na-Flow dries before applying bleach.

3. If you want the bleach to spread uncontrollably, apply
   bleach while the Dye-Na-Flow is still wet.

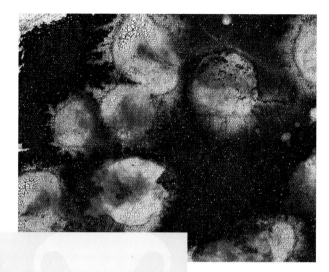

tip

Try using the Dye-Na-Flow and bleach technique
to write words or text.

TECHNIQUE

Powdered Metallic Watercolors

Powdered metallic watercolors create a soft, slightly
transparent look on fabric. A little powder goes a
long way.

1. Carefully sprinkle a small amount of powder over the
   fabric. Avoid sprinkling the powder straight from
   the jar—you'll have a hard time controlling the
   amount of powder released. Either transfer the
   powder by pinching a bit between the fingers or
   place a piece of fine netting, such as cheesecloth,
   sheer fabric, or a section of pantyhose, over the
   mouth of the jar. You can also transfer powder into a
   clean salt or pepper shaker.

2. With clean water and a brush, lightly apply water to
   the powder on the fabric. The water activates the
   powder and creates a metallic glow. The powders
   don't spread very far, so several applications might
   be necessary.

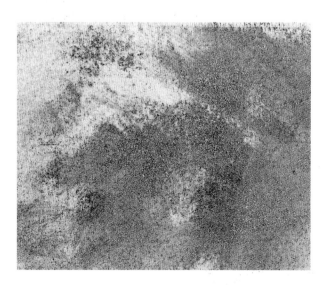

tip

Powered metallic watercolors are easy to spill, so take
care when handling the containers. Also, be sure to use
these powders in a draft-free place; they scatter easily.

Liquid Gold Leafing

Liquid leafing simulates the look of traditional leafing and is ideal for painting small accent areas with dense metallic color. The liquid starts to separate after sitting for more than 15 minutes, so shake it just before using. Because it's difficult to completely remove from the brush, you'll want to dedicate a paintbrush specifically for this product. Be sure to wipe any excess liquid from around the mouth of the jar and the lid before closing, so the lid doesn't seal itself to the jar. Liquid leafing also emits an odor, so be sure to use it in a well-ventilated area.

1. Dip a dry paintbrush into the liquid leafing and apply directly to your substrate. Avoid mixing water with this product.

2. Two applications might be needed to cover an area completely.

This example features gold leafing for the highlights of the vine/tree/leaf illustration, Caran d'Ache Neocolor II for the dark background of the house, and pastel medium for the vine illustration and background of the bird.

Pastel Medium

Pastels are an art medium in the form of a stick and consist of pure pigment combined with a binder. They have both a chalk and a crayonlike consistency and are subdivided into three types. Soft pastels are the most widely used form of pastel and have a high ratio of pigment to binder, which results in bright colors. Hard pastels have a higher ratio of binder to pigment than soft pastels. Although not as brilliant as soft pastels, they work well for creating sharp edges and fine details. Pastels with a varnished surface are considered hard pastels and are cleaner to work with than soft sticks.

Pastels are also available in pencil form. These also work well for adding fine details. Like all dry pastels, they produce a chalky dust that should be removed by turning the artwork over and gently tapping it from the back over a trash can. Never blow the excess dust from the substrate—the dust is harmful to breathe, and blowing releases it into the air. Once pastels have been applied to a surface, they are difficult to work over, unless a transparent workable fixative spray has been applied.

tip

Pastels can be messy, so wear protective clothing when working with them.

1. For large areas, rub the side of the pastel stick onto the substrate. Pastel colors can be layered, but using more than three colors in the same area can make them look muddy.

2. Blending tools, such as paper stumps, tortillons, and pastel brushes, are helpful. You can also use your fingers to blend pastels, but if you're doing a lot of blending, they can begin to hurt.

3. Seal the pastels with a transparent fixative spray in a well-ventilated area. Consider using a workable fixative, so that you can continue adding more pastels, paint, or illustrations to the piece.

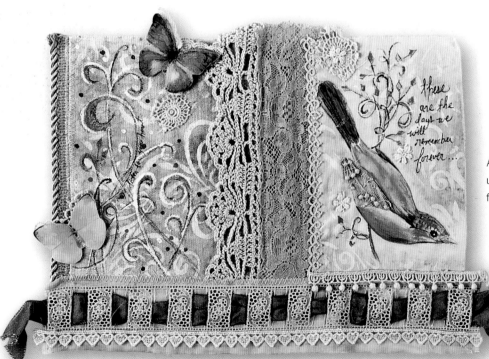

An example of the use of pastel medium for the background

Oil Pastels

Oil pastels are pastels with a waxy, crayonlike consistency. They are lightfast and rich in color.

1. For large areas, rub the side of the oil pastel stick onto substrate. You can apply oil pastel colors over each other.

2. Although oil pastels do not blend with water, they can be blended a little by rubbing them lightly with your finger or a cotton swab.

Caran d'Ache Neocolor II

Neocolor II is a line of wax-based, water-soluble pastels from Caran d'Ache. The pastels produce brilliant colors and have a softer look than colored pencils, with a greater thickness and intensity than regular crayons. They have excellent lightfastness and can be applied both wet and dry.

1. For large areas, rub the side of the crayon onto the substrate. You can apply crayon colors over each other.

2. They are easily blended with water and can be smudged with your fingers. You can also soak the fabric first and apply the crayon directly to the wet fabric as an additional blending technique.

3. A sgraffito technique can be achieved by scraping off one or more layers of color. For this technique to be successful, however, be sure to first apply several layers of color.

Crackle Paint

My experiments with crackle paint on fabric and paper have had varied results. The application instructions, and results, can vary from brand to brand. However sensitive this technique might be, it is still an excellent way to mimic the fine details of weathered wood. Whether the fine cracks produced are visible depends on the colors used for the top and bottom layers. Experiment on a piece of test material before using crackle paint in your project.

Sophisticated Finishes

Sophisticated Finishes by Modern Options is a line of solutions that create metallic finishes and antique patinas on any clean, paintable surface.

Rust Patina

Rust patina produces a reddish orange color with an opaque, gritty texture like fine sandpaper. The metallic surfacer consists of metal particles suspended in an acrylic compound.

1. Before using the rust patina, apply two coats of metallic surfacer over the designated area of your substrate. Be sure to shake the surfacer, to thoroughly combine the metal particles and the acrylic compound.

2. Allow the substrate to dry completely. To achieve a deeper rust effect (more orange or red), let the surfacer dry at least 24 hours—but not more than 36 hours—before applying the rusting solution.

3. Once the metal-painted fabric is dry, apply the rusting solution. The rust will appear gradually. It may take up to three coats to achieve the best results; however, allow at least 40 minutes between applications of rust solution. Avoid using the solution in a damp or cold environment; damp and cold prevent the coats from drying thoroughly and the patina solution from working properly.

Patina Green

Patina green produces a vibrant verdigris color with either a semitransparent or opaque density, depending on how thickly the solution is applied.

1. Apply two coats of metallic surfacer before applying the patina. Be sure to shake the surfacer, to thoroughly combine the metal particles and the acrylic compound.

2. You might need to apply several coats of the patina solution to achieve optimal results. Start by applying two or three light coats with a clean brush; as the solution begins to work, apply one last heavy coat. The final results can take up to 36 hours to fully develop.

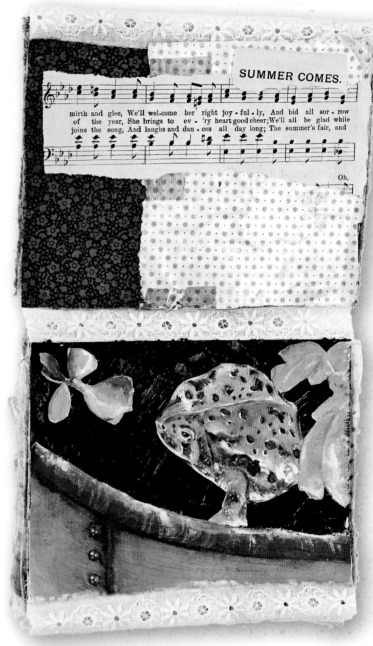

An example of the rust patina used to illustrate the bucket

Creating Projects from Nature

NOW THAT YOU HAVE learned various
techniques for gathering natural elements
and illustrating and painting from photos,
here are some ideas for using them to create
journals, pendants, and assemblages.

A journal offers a space in which you can let loose and
play, try new techniques, explore new processes, and write
personal thoughts among the pages. For centuries, artists and
scientists alike have used journals to document their lives
and the natural world. A journal also provides an opportunity
to record unique experiences when you're spending time in
nature. It serves as a snapshot in time, almost like a diary. It
can be a joy to revisit certain pages in your journals, reliving
and remembering those captured moments. Even the tiniest
flower or small, colorful leaf can spark the imagination and
produce a flurry of creative ideas. By journaling, you can hold
onto those ideas and turn them into cherished memories and
beautiful art.

Jewelry is not only a way to accent or embellish your
clothing or a special outfit, it's a wonderful way to display
your nature experiences as a wearable reminder of memories. Pendants, which are often considered small works of
art, can capture special nature moments. These tiny master-
pieces remind us to embrace the natural world.

Even an unassuming item, such as a seashell or a brightly
colored fall leaf, can hold special meaning as a remembrance
of a particular day or moment and a reminder to us that we
are all part of a larger world. Integrating these mementos into
our home and private spaces as art can often be a challenge.
Creating an assemblage with these collected items, however,
can be an excellent, artistic way to preserve them. Assemblages hold memories of not only collecting these treasures
but also of creating the special vignette within the box.

But oh, how fondly
'Tis but a little faded flower
through
many a weary year.

Creating a *Gathering Journal*

PLANTS ARE A wonderful addition to any piece of art, and gathering botanicals can be a fun activity. Unfortunately, once a plant has been cut from its stem, it begins to wither. Start the preservation process as soon as possible by carefully arranging the flower or leaf between two pieces of plain newsprint paper. The newsprint will begin absorbing moisture from the plant. Place the newsprint in a plant press to flatten the botanical and allow the plant to dry for several weeks. The pressing process removes the moisture and prevents mold from forming. It will also keep the entire cut stem intact, so that precious leaves and petals do not fall off.

Traditional plant presses come in all shapes and sizes, varying dramatically in price. One of the least expensive ways to press plants is to tuck the newsprint between the pages of a thick phone book. A phone book, however, can be difficult to carry around when you're out gathering in the woods. Even dealing with the many loose parts of a small press can be cumbersome when in the gathering process.

This journal provides nature collectors with a convenient, temporary storage space that uses glassine-envelope pages to protect those freshly cut stems. Bring it along on your nature trip, then remove the gatherings once you are home and store them in the proper manner to ensure the best drying results. Don't forget to bring a few note cards along to record information such as plant type, date, and location and to note fond memories or feelings about your experience. Tuck the cards into the front of each glassine envelope of gathered botanicals.

Materials

- cover boards measuring approximately 7¼" (18.5 cm) wide × 10" (25.4 cm) high (hard covers from a new or old book work well)
- double-sided fusible webbing for fabric
- muslin
- decorative cotton fabric
- decorative sheer fabric
- 2" (5.1 cm) ribbon
- thread to coordinate with ribbon
- sturdy piece of cardboard
- glassine envelopes
- plain newsprint paper
- dried flowers and leaves
- fabric glue
- duct tape
- sewing needle
- iron
- ironing board or pad
- ruler
- craft knife
- cutting mat
- scissors
- fine sandpaper
- ¼" (6 mm) hole punch
- ¼" (6 mm) screw posts and extensions (used in scrapbook albums)

Making the Journal Cover

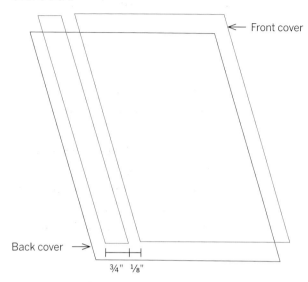

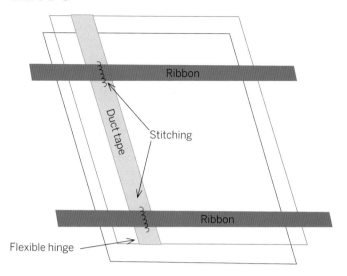

1. Cut a ¾" (1.9 cm) length from the left side of front cover board. Cut an additional ⅛" (3 mm) length from the left side of front cover board and discard.

2. Lay the ¾" (1.9 cm) cut piece and the remaining large piece of front cover board on top of the back cover, making sure both the front cover pieces and back align. There should be a ⅛" (3 mm) gap between the two front cover pieces.

3. Tear off a strip of duct tape that is twice the height of the cover boards. Be sure the tape is wide enough to connect both front cover board pieces.

4. Position the duct tape on top of the two front cover pieces and press down gently. Turn the entire front cover over to finish securing the duct tape onto the back. This creates a flexible hinge for the journal.

5. Cut a piece of fusible webbing the same size as the duct tape hinge. Remove one side of the wax paper from the fusible webbing and place the webbing on top of the duct tape. Follow the directions on the fusible webbing package to secure this piece to the duct tape. Remove the remaining wax paper from the secured fusible webbing.

6. Cut a piece of decorative cotton fabric the same size as the duct tape hinge. Place the fabric on top of the fusible webbing. Secure the fabric in place with an iron.

7. Punch a hole in the left side of the front and back cover boards, approximately 5⁄16" (8 mm) from the edge. Repeat. Two holes per cover are sufficient, although you might want to make more.

8. Cut two pieces of 2" (5.1 cm) -wide ribbon three times the length of the journal.

9. Find the center point of each cut ribbon piece. Sew ½" (1.3 cm) from the top and bottom edges of the front cover board through the flexible hinge along the ⅛" (3 mm) gap between the two front cover pieces.

Making the Decorative Frame for the Cover

STEPS 1–7

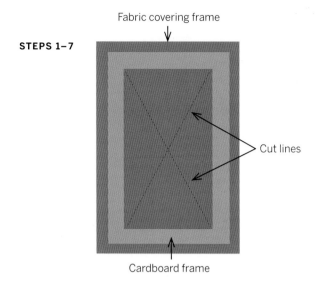

Fabric covering frame

Cut lines

Cardboard frame

Consider dying or staining your muslin fabric before using it. You can also write your favorite poem or inspirational phrase around the edge of the fabric frame with a permanent marker.

1. Cut a piece of sturdy cardboard one half the size of the front cover board.

2. Cut a window into the cardboard, leaving a ½" (1.3 cm) frame on all sides.

3. Cut a piece of muslin fabric the same size as the cardboard frame, plus an additional ⅛" (3 mm) on all sides.

4. Cut a piece of fusible webbing the same size as the muslin fabric. Remove one side of the wax paper from the fusible webbing. Place the fusible webbing on top of the muslin fabric and iron it onto the fabric. Remove the remaining wax paper from the secured fusible webbing.

5. Position the muslin fabric, fusible webbing side down, on top of the cardboard frame. Position it so the fabric overlaps ⅛" (3 mm) on all sides. Iron muslin fabric to the frame.

6. Cut an X in the muslin fabric inside the window of the cardboard frame.

7. Wrap all edges around the frame. Trim the excess muslin fabric and secure in place with the iron.

Down the lane and up th

Creating a Window for Pressed Botanicals

1. Cut two pieces of decorative sheer fabric ⅛" (3 mm) smaller than the outside edge of the cardboard frame.

2. Cut a piece of fusible webbing the same size as the decorative sheer fabric.

3. Remove one side of the wax paper from the fusible webbing and place the webbing on the front side of the bottom piece of decorative sheer fabric. Iron fusible webbing to the decorative sheer fabric.

4. Remove the remaining wax paper from the secured fusible webbing. Arrange dried botanicals on top of webbing.

5. Position the top piece of decorative sheer fabric over the botanicals and secure the two decorative sheer fabrics together with an iron.

Putting the Pieces Together

1. Trace the inside window of the fabric-covered cardboard frame onto the center of the front cover board.

2. Cut the traced shape from the book cover and sand the rough edges of the cutout.

3. Adhere the botanical window piece to the front cover board over the cutout with fabric glue.

4. Adhere the fabric-covered cardboard frame to the front cover board over the window piece with fabric glue. Allow the glue to dry.

5. Punch holes that correspond to the holes in the cover boards into the glassine envelopes.

6. Thread the screw posts through the cover boards and envelopes.

7. Fold pieces of plain newsprint paper and tuck into each glassine envelope page.

Avoid using bridal tulle or a sheer fabric with sizable holes. Consider using a sheer fabric with a pattern or sparkles to add interest. Avoid using excessive heat and pressure with the iron when securing fusible webbing to sheer fabrics—your fabric and dried botanicals will pucker.

GATHERING FLOWERS AND LEAVES

- Pick plants in the middle of day, when the petals and leaves are the least damp.

- Gently shake the plant to remove bugs.

- The look of the plant when pressed will be the same as it was when picked. Botanicals chosen during midday will have open petals.

- If picking a plant that is already on the ground, choose one from the top of a pile or that has had the least amount of exposure to moisture.

- Press plants of similar thickness together, to ensure thorough, even drying.

- Flowers in the early blooming stages have the most vibrant colors.

- Fall is a wonderful time for drying leaves. Note that some leaves change color as they age.

- Be sure to use fresh newsprint paper each time you gather botanicals.

POEM,

CONTENTS

SUMMER IN THE PASTURES

ALONG

JUNE.

NATURE RAMBLES

These pages consist of bark cloth fabric stitched to water-color paper. Vintage photo pages are adhered on top with gel medium. The blue jays are painted on muslin fabric and embellished with lace using techniques in chapter 2.

Creating a *Seasons Journal*

A FAVORITE WAY to remember the year is by looking at it through the contrasts of the seasons. Each season brings new experiences: the first snowfall of winter, the bright, budding flowers and trees of spring, the warm temperatures and fresh fruit of summer, the colorful foliage of fall.

Using the seasons as a starting point for journaling helps break up the daunting task of capturing a whole year into manageable projects. You can combine a year's worth of art in one book or create four separate books. Creating a book for each season gives you clear stopping and starting points and provides a single main focus. You also have closure from one season to the next, by finishing a book, setting it aside, and beginning anew.

There are a number of methods for binding journals, but for this particular project, I use an altered accordion binding, which allows you to add as many pages as you want to a particular book.

Painted daffodils on muslin are accented by dyed fabrics and vintage laces sewn to a watercolor paper substrate.

The peach, bowl, and the bird are painted on muslin fabric. The shadows under the bowl and peach are represented with torn paper from a vintage textbook. Cotton fabrics are stitched to the background.

Materials

- cover boards (such as hard covers from a new or old book)
- double-sided fusible webbing for fabric (optional)
- 200 thread-count bleached muslin fabric
- decorative cotton fabrics
- decorative sheer fabrics
- 2" (5.1-cm) -wide lace or fabric
- 1 yard (.9 m) of ribbon to coordinate with the book cover and/or particular season
- acrylic paint
- 300-lb. (640-gsm) watercolor paper
- heavy gel medium
- 1" (2.5 cm) sponge brush for applying gel medium

- miscellaneous ephemera
- miscellaneous decorative papers
- miscellaneous stencils
- miscellaneous fabric inks and dyes
- light box
- mechanical pencil with a fine tip
- white eraser
- #1 and #3 round paintbrushes
- 1" (2.5 cm) flat paintbrush
- paint palette
- water cup
- rag for cleaning brushes

- scissors
- small embroidery scissors
- craft knife
- ruler
- cutting pad
- fine sandpaper
- sewing needle and thread to coordinate (optional)
- sewing machine (optional)
- iron (optional)
- ironing board or pad (optional)

Making the Journal Cover

1. Remove the spine and pages from a selected hard-back book and set aside. Consider choosing books related to nature and, more specifically, the season. Interesting vintage books can be found in antique stores, flea markets, or online auctions.

2. Lightly sand the rough edges of the cover boards.

3. Alter the outside of the covers using distressing techniques and finishes, paint, stencils, and miscellaneous ephemera. Here, white acrylic paint and a flourish stencil were used with layered washes of walnut inks to soften the dramatic contrast of white against the green cover. (See chapter 2, page 48, for instructions on distressing fabric and paper.)

4. Consider finishing the cover boards by covering the raw edges with a decorative fabric. Here, thin strips of dupioni silk were glued to the edges of the covers. The same fabric and stencil treatment was used to give all the journals a cohesive look on the outside, despite the contrasting, seasonal pages on the inside.

5. For the journal closure, vintage metal photo album hinges were glued to the front and a ribbon was drawn through a hole on one edge of each hinge. You can also wrap a plain ribbon around the book or use a stretchy cord looped around a button as a closure.

Creating the Pages

1. Using a book page as a template, cut pieces of watercolor paper. These are your journal pages.

2. Cut strips of 2" (5.1 cm) -wide lace or fabric the same height as the page template. You should have one strip per page, except for the last page in the book. The fabric strips form the folds of the book and hold the pages together.

3. To create the accordion folds, adhere each 2" (5.1 cm) strip of lace or fabric to the back left side of each page using matte gel medium. Do this for every page you add to the journal, except for the last page of the journal.

Decorating the Pages

1. Although it is perfectly acceptable to record each nature experience on a new page, you can also create a page spread. As you add pages to your book, the accordion folds will zigzag from front to back. A spread is considered two single pages along with the fold or 2" (5.1 cm) strip of lace.

2. Start by sketching and painting the nature subjects for the page spread. (See chapter 2, page 40, for instructions on painting on muslin.) Be sure to use a substrate that allows the subject to be cut from the original background.

3. Once the painting is dry, cut the subject from the background with a small pair of embroidery scissors. The embroidery scissors will help you to maneuver around tight corners.

4. Decorate the page with a collage of materials, such as fabric or decorative papers, that relate to your experience and to the subject. Use gel medium or stitching to attach objects to the page in a layering process. Consider using stitching for both decorative and construction purposes. Remember that using contrasting colors for the background will make the painted subject stand out; analogous colors make the subject blend into the background.

   Many of the journal pages featured in this book display a combination of subjects painted on muslin fabric, a mix of decorative and distressed fabrics, miscellaneous papers, flat ephemera, and stitching. The main subjects were painted with acrylic paint and cut out with a pair of small, very sharp scissors. Find more samples from *Seasons Journal* in the gallery, which begins on page 84.

5. Attach the painted subjects to the page with matte gel medium.

The heart weaves a
nest of dreams, of wishes
as the light slips away
into a starry sky
at the turning of time
at the edge of life
the soul never fades
it will always
Burn Bright

Creating *Painted Pendants*

I HAVE ALWAYS HAD an affinity for small works of art. The idea of creating a piece that requires the viewer to come close to appreciate the details is something that appeals to my artistic muse. This love for small art also extends to a love of jewelry, in particular, beautiful pendants. I am fascinated by the way a pendant can tell a story and provide clues about its owner within such a tiny space.

Creating nature-inspired jewelry opens up a whole new realm of possibilities. We can capture cherished moments and transform them into wearable memories. The same nature images we use to make large painted artworks can be used to create beautiful and unusual jewelry pieces. By reducing the desired image or cropping in on a particular area of a photo, you instantly have a suitable subject at the perfect size for a pendant. Be judicious when choosing the size of your pendant. Anything over 4" (10.2 cm) wide can look oversize and garish when worn around the neck.

Painted Fabric Portrait Pendant

A standard pendant shape, such as a square, rectangle, circle, or oval, can make a pendant seem more like a larger work of art that might hang on the wall and works well when you want to capture the essence of a scene or present a subject as a portrait. The head and upper body of an animal or a flower with a few leaves provides enough subject matter to create a 3" or 4" (7.6 or 10.2 cm) pendant that contains a fair amount of detail. As with painting a larger work, it is not necessary to render every detail for the viewer to understand the picture. In addition to painting the pendant, consider adding embellishments, such as beads, trim, lace, or even a vintage brooch, to the finished piece.

Materials

- unwashed white muslin fabric (200 thread count)
- decorative fabric to coordinate with the painting
- leather cording (2 mm size)
- heavy white felt
- vintage pin (optional)
- acrylic paints
- double-sided fusible webbing for fabric
- thread to coordinate with the painting
- #3 and #5 round paintbrush
- mechanical pencil with 0.5 lead
- clean white eraser
- paint palette
- water cup
- rag for cleaning brushes
- wire cutters used for jewelry (optional)
- scissors
- sewing needle
- sewing machine (optional)
- iron
- ironing board or pad
- ruler

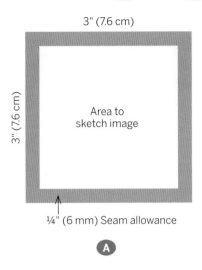

3" (7.6 cm)

3" (7.6 cm)

Area to
sketch image

¼" (6 mm) Seam allowance

A

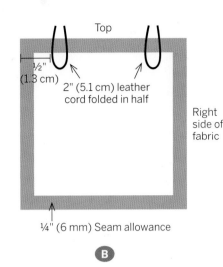

Top

½"
(1.3 cm)

2" (5.1 cm) leather
cord folded in half

Right
side of
fabric

¼" (6 mm) Seam allowance

B

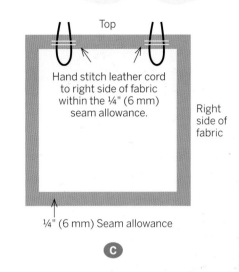

Top

Hand stitch leather cord
to right side of fabric
within the ¼" (6 mm)
seam allowance.

Right
side of
fabric

¼" (6 mm) Seam allowance

C

Painting the Portrait

1. Transfer a photo or copyright-free image onto a piece of white copy paper. The copy paper image should be approximately 30 percent lighter than the original. (See chapter 2, page 34, for instructions on transferring images for photocopying.)

2. Cut a piece of unwashed muslin to the desired size.

3. With a pencil, lightly mark on the backside of the muslin a ¼" (6 mm) seam allowance on all sides.

4. Sketch out the image on the cut muslin piece inside the area marked for the seam allowance (A).

5. Paint the image following the directions for Painting Nature on Muslin, page 40.

Creating the Pendant

1. When the painting is completely dry, cut a piece of decorative fabric the same size as the muslin piece.

2. Cut a piece of white felt the same size as the muslin minus the seam allowance.

3. Cut a piece of fusible webbing the same size as the felt. Remove one side of the wax paper from the fusible webbing and place the webbing onto the felt. Follow the directions on the fusible webbing package to secure the webbing to the felt. Remove the remaining wax paper from the secured fusible webbing.

4. Position the felt, fusible-webbing side down, within the marked pencil lines on the back of the painted muslin. Iron the felt to the back of the muslin.

Assembling the Necklace

1. Cut two 2" (5.1 cm) pieces of leather cording. Fold each piece in half.

2. Position each piece of folded leather cording at the top on the painted side of the muslin. The outside edge of each leather piece should be ½" (1.3 cm) from each edge of the muslin. Vertically, the leather cording should cross through the seam allowance and into the image area. Make sure the fold of the cord is pointed downward and extends only ½" (1.3 cm) over the seam allowance line into the image area (B).

3. Hand stitch each cord to the muslin, making sure to stitch in the ¼" (6 mm) seam allowance area (C).

4. Position the painted muslin side and the right side of the decorative fabric together. The cording should be sandwiched between the two pieces. Sew both sides and the top together, leaving the bottom of the pendant open. Trim any excess fabric from the seams.

5. Turn the sewed pendant inside out, so that the painting and two leather loops are now showing on the outside. Fold under the raw edges on the bottom of the pendant and sew the pendant closed.

6. Cut a 30" (76.2 cm) -long piece of leather cording and string it though the leather loops at the top of the pendant.

7. If desired, embellish the pendant with a vintage pin. Remove the pin back with wire cutters and adhere the pin to the pendant with industrial-strength adhesive.

Beaded Fabric Pendant Necklace

The advantage of using muslin as a substrate in mixed-media artwork is that it is flexible. This advantage quickly becomes a disadvantage, however, when you want to make a pendant that needs to be flat and stiff.

With the portrait pendant, this stiffness was achieved by sewing together multiple layers of fabric. This method is difficult to use, however, when you're working with irregular shapes. For this pendant, we apply a layer of material often used to help ball caps retain their shape, to create irregularly shaped pendants that are stiff enough to use for any necklace.

Materials

- unwashed white muslin fabric (200 thread count)
- 1 or 2 strands small- to medium-size decorative beads to coordinate with painting
- 1 or 2 strands small filler beads
- 1 roll medium stringing wire
- #1 size crimp beads
- 1 toggle clasp
- Pellon Peltex double-sided fusible webbing
- acrylic paints
- #1 and #3 round paintbrushes
- mechanical pencil with 0.5 lead
- clean white eraser
- paint palette
- water cup
- rag for cleaning brushes
- wire cutters used for jewelry
- crimp bead tool
- small pair of sharp embroidery scissors
- iron
- ironing board or pad

Painting the Pendant

1. Transfer a photo or copyright-free image no larger than 4" (10.2 cm) onto a piece of white copy paper. The copy paper image should be approximately 30 percent lighter than the original. (See chapter 2, page 34, for instructions on transferring images for photocopying.)

2. Cut two pieces of unwashed muslin approximately the same size as the image.

3. Sketch out the image on one of the cut pieces of muslin.

4. Paint the image following the directions for Painting Nature on Muslin, page 40.

Creating the Pendant

1. When the painting is completely dry, cut a piece of Pellon Peltex the same size as the painted muslin.

2. Follow the directions on the package to secure the Pellon Peltex to the back of the muslin.

3. Distress the second piece of muslin following your preferred method. (See Distressing Techniques for Backgrounds, page 48.)

4. Cut a strand of stringing wire to the desired length. Remember to take into consideration the addition of a toggle clasp at either end of the strand.

5. Once the distressed muslin is completely dry, position the wire horizontally across the back of the pendant, so it rests on the Pellon Peltex secured to the back of the painted muslin. Be sure to leave an equal amount of wire on each side of the pendant (D).

6. Place the distressed muslin on top of the Pellon Peltex and the positioned wire and secure with an iron.

**STEP 5,
CREATING THE PENDANT**

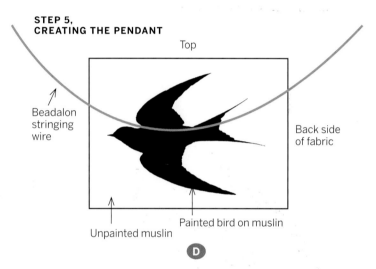

Top

Beadalon stringing wire

Back side of fabric

Painted bird on muslin

Unpainted muslin

D

7. Carefully extract the painted image from the muslin using the embroidery scissors. Be sure not to cut the stringing wire when extracting the painted image from the background. When cutting close to the wire, cut the top layer with the painted subject and Pellon Peltex separately from the bottom layer of distressed muslin.

Assembling the Necklace

1. Thread beads onto the remaining wire, alternating decorative beads and filler beads.

2. Once the desired number of beads has been added, thread a crimp bead onto each end of the wire.

3. Thread one part of the toggle clasp onto each end, after the crimp bead. Loop the remaining wire around the clasp ring and thread it back through the crimp bead.

4. Using the crimp bead tool, close the crimp bead to hold the wire securely. Trim excess wire.

Creating *Nature Assemblages*

WHO CAN RESIST PICKING UP a colorful fall leaf that floats to the ground and lands at your feet, gathering twigs that cast an interesting shadow when the sun shines on them, collecting brilliant shells uncovered by the tide on a sandy beach, or saving a bird's nest blown from a tree during a storm? What do we do with these collections that build up and get shuffled from room to room? Often, they simply gather dust in the corner or, worse, are tucked away in a box and forgotten.

An ideal way to organize and display those nature gems is to incorporate them into meaningful and interesting assemblages. An assemblage is a collection of various materials that have been combined to create an artistic composition. With the correct tools and materials, you, too, can create lasting memories from your nature gatherings.

Materials

- collected nature elements
- vintage or worn book covers and pages
- Thin sheets of patina metal or metal mesh
- miscellaneous ephemera (metal charms, soldered charms, nature photos and illustrations, vintage photo album pages, other decorations related to nature)
- mat board
- industrial-strength craft adhesive (such as E6000)
- heavy gel medium
- brush for applying gel medium
- toothpicks

- heavy thread (optional)
- sewing needle (optional)
- mechanical pencil
- metal ruler with cork backing
- craft knife
- Japanese screw punch (optional)
- rag for cleaning
- scissors
- small wire cutter

Choosing a Frame

Start by choosing the right frame to hold and protect your artwork. Measure the depth of the elements you want to incorporate into your three-dimensional collage and use the greatest depth as your guide. If you're unsure of the elements you want to use, set a reasonable maximum depth before you start shopping for a frame and stick to it.

Most craft stores carry standard-size frames and shadowboxes. Occasionally, you can find interesting and unusual frames or shallow shadowboxes at discount retailers or closeout chains, so be sure to shop around. Standard-size, ready-made frames are more convenient and less expensive than custom frames, which can sometimes take weeks to have made.

Of course, a shadowbox does not have to come from a craft store. Other boxes, such as wooden cigar boxes, for example, can make excellent assemblage frames. Just remove the lid and attach a piece of clear acrylic to the rim of the box to protect your delicate natural elements. Be sure that the outside support you choose for your assemblage is sturdy and surrounds the nature collage completely.

Other options for assemblage frames include vintage wooden cheese boxes or, for larger collages, even wooden crates. These make interesting substitutes for standard frames because they are much deeper and sometimes unusual in size. If you choose one of these alternatives, be sure to decorate the box before placing your assemblage inside. If you plan to hang the assemblage on the wall, remember to add picture-framing hardware to the back of the box before putting your artwork inside. Always cover the box opening with acrylic or glass to protect the contents from damage and dust.

Another idea is to create your assemblage inside a clear container, such as a glass jar or canister. Elements can be free-floating or secured with adhesive, depending on where the artwork is displayed.

Use a sharp craft knife when cutting mat board. Because it has such a dense composition, an accurate, clean cut is difficult to achieve with scissors, which can leave a jagged edge. To cut mat board with a craft knife, use a metal ruler with cork backing to prevent slippage. Place the ruler on the edge being cut, and hold it firmly. With the craft knife in your other hand, make an incision, using the ruler as a sturdy brace to guide your knife. You'll need to use some pressure. If the mat board is particularly thick, you will probably have to cut more than once to slice completely through it. Be sure to hold the ruler firmly in place, and keep cutting until the board is cut through.

Selecting a Substrate

Once you've chosen your frame, you'll need a substrate—every assemblage needs a sturdy background. Mat board works well because, although it is relatively thin, it has a dense composition, which makes it sturdy. Also, unlike the background of a painting, which is often painted, an assemblage substrate is generally left natural, and mat board, in addition to being sturdy, creates a border around the art. When choosing mat board, select a light color. Light background colors help neutralize shadows, which can increase as the depth of the frame increases, and illuminate the work. White is the best color for reflecting light.

Once you have chosen your substrate, you'll need to cut it to fit the frame. Measure the height and width of the inside area of the frame and cut the substrate to size. If you're using a frame purchased from the store, take the backing off and determine the inside dimensions. Test the cut piece for accuracy by fitting it into the opening. It should fit snugly into the frame.

Planning the Composition

Before tacking your elements into place on the mat board substrate, plan your composition, so you have a clear idea of how the work will come together. It's not uncommon for little surprises—albeit sometimes good ones—to happen in the final construction. Planning helps prevent major mishaps when you're ready to adhere the assemblage in place.

1. Begin by gathering all the tools and materials. Collect more materials and ephemera than you think you will use, so that you have plenty of options to choose from during the design phase.

2. If you plan to include patina metal in the artwork, antique all your pieces before beginning the design. Because no two pieces come out exactly the same during the patina process, some might have better color or more interesting textures than others making them better suited for the assemblage.

3. Before using any natural elements in an assemblage, be sure they are properly cleaned and preserved (see page 20). You don't want your nature materials to crumble or turn an unexpected color.

Building the Design

Once you have gathered your materials for the assemblage, experiment with potential arrangements by creating layers of objects on the substrate. You might overlap materials and add or subtract certain elements as you develop the composition.

1. Place the mat board substrate onto your work surface and cover it with white card stock. The card stock protects the clean mat board while you are experimenting with an arrangement of elements. Be sure the card stock is the same size as the substrate, so you have an accurate size guide and can trim or edit materials that extend past the edges.

2. When building the design, consider starting with a layer of book covers, book or magazine pages, or metal or metal mesh sheets, as shown in the photograph below. Use varying sizes to add interest, and think about staggering the arrangement by having some overlapping elements hang over the edges of those underneath.

3. Once you have a layer of larger materials on the bottom, create your focal point by adding natural elements, such as large leaves, a bundle of small twigs, an interesting branch, or long grasses to the background. Be sensitive to the way the colors of the natural materials reflect against and contrast with the background. Some colors are so subtle that they simply fade away when placed onto another area of color. Use materials that blend well but don't disappear when lying against one another.

4. Don't be afraid to allow the large natural elements to extend to the edges of the mat substrate. Use scissors or small wire cutters to trim pieces that extend beyond the substrate boundaries.

5. Prune any elements that exceed the maximum depth of the frame. You can push the boundaries a little if you're working with pliable materials, but stiff, unyielding elements can be compacted and shifted in the frame by the glass or acrylic cover.

6. Continue building your design with additional materials and ephemera. Place the main subject of the piece—a bird's nest, large seashell, or other important element—on the top layer. Once the main subject has been positioned, add more ephemera to complement it and help move the viewer's eye around the entire composition. Avoid placing elements into the design that obstruct the view of the main subject or draw attention from it.

7. It is easy to add too many elements to the assemblage. A "less-is-more" approach can be quite beautiful. Don't let the natural elements be overwhelmed by too many manmade items or other natural elements that vie for attention.

Finalizing the Composition

1. When you have constructed an arrangement that is pleasing, carefully move the card stock with the assemblage arrangement off the mat board underneath and sweep into the trash any miscellaneous waste, shavings, and pieces that have shed from natural materials.

2. Consider taking a quick photo of the arranged assemblage and printing a copy of it for reference as you adhere the pieces into place. If you choose not to take a photo, be sure to study your arrangement carefully so that you can recreate it on the mat board substrate.

3. Working from the bottom up, use industrial-strength adhesive to connect the background elements to the substrate and to each other. Use an adhesive that dries slowly, so you have time to make adjustments and move the materials into the correct position.

A finished composition
after all items are adhered

tip

E6000 has a gummy consistency and can be easily removed when wet. If the adhesive seeps out from under a material and can be seen in the collage, use toothpicks to immediately remove it before it hardens.

Framing the Assemblage

When the glue has thoroughly dried, you are ready to place your completed assemblage in the frame.

1. Clean the inside glass and allow it to dry. Clean the inside walls of the shadowbox frame with a dusting cloth.

2. Although most of the elements should not move if they were adhered with industrial-strength adhesive, avoid holding the artwork with the elements facing the floor. If a particular material does not hold, reapply adhesive to the loose element and allow the entire piece to dry for another 24 hours.

3. Once all the elements are secure, carefully place the artwork into the back of the frame, bottom edge first. Try to avoid holding the frame and artwork in a vertical position until the work is securely in the frame. Expect some small bits to float to the bottom of the shadowbox as the natural materials continue to shed.

4. Replace the frame backing and secure.

4. You can use the industrial adhesive to adhere large leaves, bundled twigs, branches, and grasses to background pieces, as long as it doesn't show. Be sure to apply it to the back of the elements or cover the glued areas with other materials. If additional materials will not cover the glue, consider attaching the elements by drilling (or punching) holes through the background and substrate and sewing them down or using wire to hold them. Visible stitching or wire can add an unexpected, yet interesting texture to the artwork.

   Only a small amount of glue is needed to adhere elements such as leaves. Heavier items need more. Materials that span the entire length of the substrate might need to be held in place with a combination of adhesive and sewing or wiring.

5. Continue attaching the remaining elements to the collage.

6. Once all the elements are in place, move the finished artwork (making sure to keep the substrate horizontal) to a place in which it will not be disturbed for at least 24 hours. This will give the adhesive time to dry and harden.

Final framed assemblage

Gallery of Nature Inspired Art

THE IDEAS, PHOTOGRAPHS, artworks, and techniques in the preceding chapters are designed to guide you through the process of creating your own nature-inspired art. The Gallery is all about inspiration. It's an opportunity for me to share other works that use several of the ideas and techniques discussed in this book. The painting here, for example, began with an illustration on muslin fabric; the bird was then painted and its wings embellished with laces. The background was distressed with walnut inks, and bits of assemblage were added to create a completed piece.

Enormous possibilities abound when creating mixed-media art—the number of materials and techniques you can use seem endless. Sometimes, having these endless possibilities can cause confusion and hesitation—how do you choose just the right elements to include or the best technique to use when rendering a subject and background? The answer is to listen to your inner voice. Tap into your own likes and dislikes about particular colors, techniques, styles, and subjects. That voice can give your work direction by letting your personal style shine through.

Each of my works embraces fundamental feelings regarding my joy of life, my love of home, and my enormous adoration of nature. Spending time with nature and being engaged in the moment can truly be life altering. Nature has helped me escape from the frantic and often hectic pace of daily corporate responsibilities. I am sincerely grateful for every step I have taken on this journey and for my discovery of the natural world. That gratitude has, in turn, revealed itself in my life as an outpouring of art, which has provided opportunities to create some of my most unforgettable and cherished experiences. I hope these works inspire you to create your own wonderful memories.

Turn me loose and let me be
Young once more and fancy free;
Let me wander where I will,
Down the lane and up the hill.

A combination of techniques, Dyeing with Instant Tea, Walnut Ink Crystals, Walnut Ink Sprays, and Caran d'Ache Neocolor II, from chapter 2 pages, 48, 49, and 53 were used to create the varied background of this artwork. The butterfly and foliage were illustrated using the Painting Nature on Muslin technique from chapter 2.

This little songbird was painted on muslin. Words from
a vintage textbook were added using gel medium. The
entire artwork was placed in a vintage swing frame.

Both pyramid shaped pincushions are constructed from cotton fabrics with a bird painted on muslin fabric stitched to the front panel. Each pincushion is stuffed with polyester fiberfill to help give the structure shape. Lavender potpourri is added to the inside for weight and to keep the pyramid upright.

Pages from the *Season Journals—Nature Rambles Spring to Summer* are a
collage of paper, fabric, and miscellaneous ephemera. The nature subjects were illustrated and painted. Each collage element was attached to
a thick piece of watercolor paper using decorative stitching. A piece of
vintage lace serves as the hinge in this accordion journal.

A page spread from the *Season Journals—Nature Rambles Spring to Summer* combines embroidered fabric, gesso vintage book pages, and a paper napkin with a large floral print. Included in this collage are a teapot and bird in flight painted on muslin fabric. Elements were attached using gel medium.

Another page spread from the *Season Journals—Nature Rambles Spring to Summer* was constructed by painting a heavy wash of acrylic paint on watercolor paper, adding vintage papers, and linen fabric on top, along with a teacup and bird in flight painted on muslin fabric. Elements were adhered to the painted page using gel medium and stitching.

Two layers of sheer material were stitched to a white watercolor paper background. The robin sitting among the holly foliage was painted on muslin. These pages are from the *Season Journals—Nature Rambles Winter to Spring.*

The background for these pages is watercolor paper painted in a blue wash of acrylics. Handwriting was added to the painted background providing a bit of texture to an otherwise plain canvas. A vintage handkerchief is split into two halves and stitched to both sides of the page spread. A vintage brooch and belt buckle are glued on top using industrial-strength adhesive. The bird on the branch was painted on muslin.

SLAYER of winter, art thou here again?
O welcome, thou that bring'st the summer nigh!
The bitter wind makes not thy victory vain,
Nor will we mock thee for thy faint blue sky.
Welcome, O March! whose kindly days and dry,
Make April ready for the throstle's song,
Thou first redresser of the winter's wrong!

Yea, welcome, March! and though I die ere June,
Yet for the hope of life I give thee praise,
Striving to swell the burden of the tune
That even now I hear thy brown birds raise.

MARCH.

These pages are from the *Season Journals—Nature Rambles Summer to Fall*. A close-up section of a rusty bucket was sketched onto watercolor paper. The side and lip of the pail were distressed using the Instant Tea and Sophisticated Finishes techniques, pages 48 and 54. Copper brads were added to the side of the bucket with industrial-strength adhesive to represent metal rivets. Extra-course pumice gel was mixed with Walnut Crystals to create the lumpy texture of real dirt where the toad is sitting.

This page spread is from the *Season Journals—Nature Rambles Summer to Fall*. The floral print graphic is extracted from a preprinted cotton fabric and attached to the page using gel medium. Paper scraps from miscellaneous books represent the shadows located under the painted bird and flower graphic. The background wallpaper and tabletop are cotton fabrics stitched to watercolor paper.

The butterfly sitting on the purple flower is painted on fabric. Crocheted flowers and leaves cut from a vintage tea towel were attached with gel medium to this page from the *Season Journal—Nature Rambles Summer to Fall*.

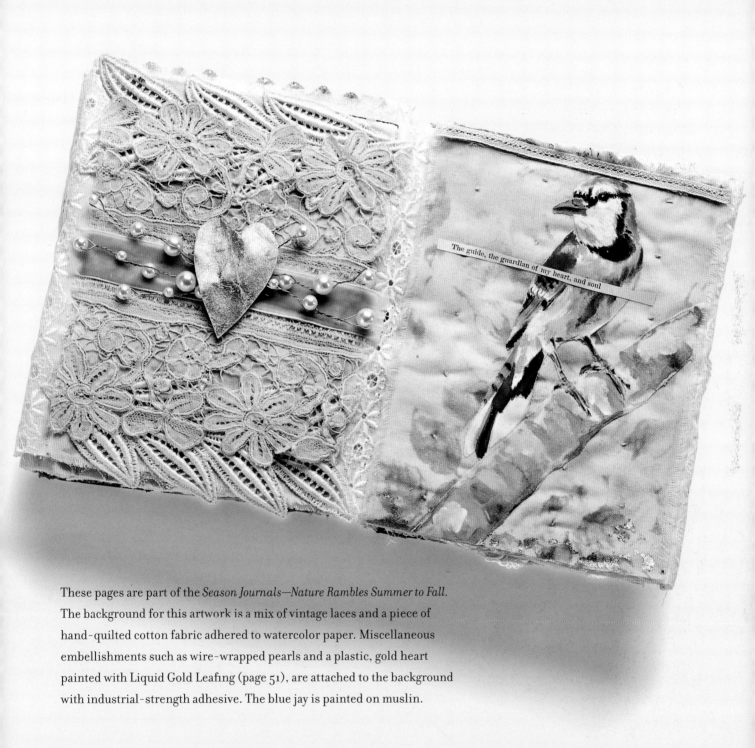

The guide, the guardian of my heart, and soul

These pages are part of the *Season Journals—Nature Rambles Summer to Fall*.
The background for this artwork is a mix of vintage laces and a piece of
hand-quilted cotton fabric adhered to watercolor paper. Miscellaneous
embellishments such as wire-wrapped pearls and a plastic, gold heart
painted with Liquid Gold Leafing (page 51), are attached to the background
with industrial-strength adhesive. The blue jay is painted on muslin.

Collaged elements such as vintage papers, old stamps, damask
fabric, and antique lace were stitched to the background of these
pages in the *Season Journals—Nature Rambles Winter to Spring*.
A rhinestone brooch adds a bit of sparkle. The barn swallow is
painted on muslin and has lace embellishments. A dried piece
of foliage was also included in this spread.

The background for these pages is a photo paper transfer to fabric that is stitched to watercolor paper. An overlay of sparkle bridal tulle and larger felt snowflakes were added to the scene representing winter. The cardinal is painted on muslin.

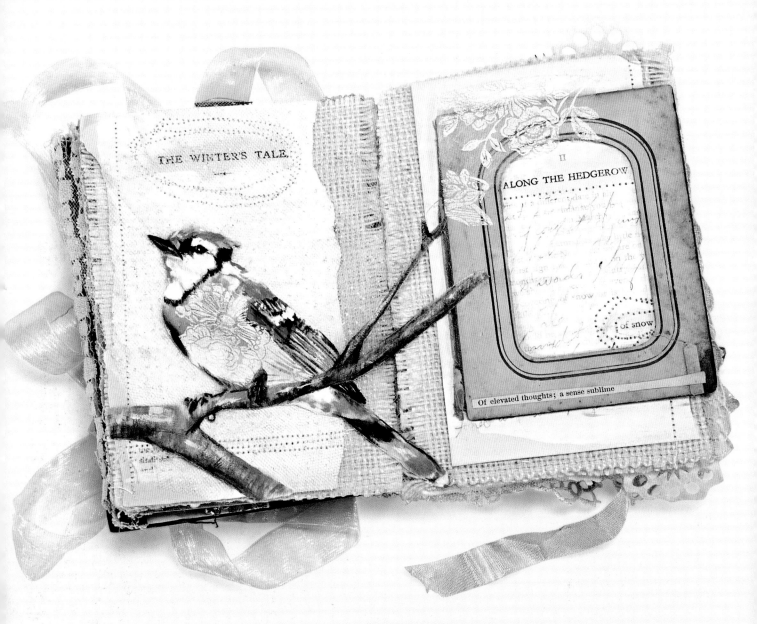

Bleached burlap is the foundation for this page spread in the *Season Journals—Nature Rambles Winter to Spring*. Pages from a book on Shakespeare were painted with a white acrylic wash and stitched on top. The blue jay is painted on muslin fabric and embellished.

Multiple pieces of antique lace were stitched to dark gray painted watercolor paper. Small branches were dried and attached to the page with wire. Each twig was wrapped with clear beads. A vintage belt buckle, vintage paper, and a metal heart crest were attached with industrial-strength adhesive.

Resources ❧

Australia

ECKERSLEY'S ART & CRAFT
www.eckersleys.com.au

Canada

CURRY'S ART STORE
www.currys.com
art and craft supplies

LAZAR STUDIOWERX INC
www.lazarstudiowerx.com
rubber stamps, art tools

France

GRAPHIGRO
www.graphigro.com
art supplies

Italy

VERTECCI
www.vertecchi.com
design and art supplies

United Kingdom

CREATIVE CRAFTS
www.creativecrafts.co.uk
art and craft supplies

HOBBYCRAFT GROUP LIMITED
www.hobbycraft.co.uk
art and craft supplies

JOHN LEWIS
www.johnlewis.co.uk
art and craft supplies

T N LAWRENCE & SON LTD.
www.lawrence.co.uk
art supplies

United States

A.C. MOORE
www.acmoore.com
art and craft supplies

ARCHIVER'S
www.archiversonline.com
scrapbook and collage supplies

DANIEL SMITH
www.danielsmith.com
general art supplies, powdered metallic watercolors

DHARMA TRADING COMPANY
www.dharmatrading.com
specialty fabric supplies, Dye-Na-Flow, fabric inks, dyes

DICK BLICK
www.dickblick.com
general art supplies, NaturePrint Paper, printmaking inks, Caran d'Ache Neocolor II crayons, artist tape, oil pastel sticks, art pastel sticks, canvases

FIRE MOUNTAIN GEMS
www.firemountaingems.com
general jewelry supplies, leather cording, beads, stringing wire

HOBBY LOBBY
www.hobbylobby.com
general art supplies, mat board, watercolor paper, plain newsprint paper

JO-ANN FABRIC AND CRAFT STORES
www.joann.com
general sewing supplies, 200 thread count muslin, embroidery scissors, double-sided fusible webbing for fabric, Pellon Peltex double-sided fusible webbing

KINKO'S
www.kinkos.com
copy services

Michaels
www.michaels.com
general art supplies, gel medium, charcoal sticks, acrylic paint, acrylic medium, paintbrushes, brayer, light box, graphite paper, fine sandpaper, liquid gold leafing, crackle paint, fabric glue, scrapbook album screw posts, stencils, decorative papers, wire cutter for jewelry, crimp beads, crimp tool, beads

Modern Options
www.modernoptions.com
patina solutions

Mother Rubber Art Stamps
www.motherrubber.com
Tsukineko Walnut Inks and Sprays

Nashville Wraps
www.nashvillewraps.com
glassine envelopes

Sargent-Welch
www.sargentwelch.com
botany press

Volcano Arts
www.volcanoarts.biz
rubber mallet, hole punch, Japanese screw punch, heavy linen thread

Wal-Mart
www.walmart.com
general office supplies, supplies for gathering natural objects, press-and-seal plastic wrap, Styrofoam plates, tweezers, instant tea, bleach pen, duct tape

About the Author

TRACIE LYN HUSKAMP holds a degree in graphic design with an emphasis in fine art. Her passion for mixed media and collage fuels the fires of her creative spirit and continues to lead her on a wondrous journey of artistic and self-discovery.

Tracie's mixed-media work has received both regional and national recognition. Her art was published on the cover and in a feature article in the July/August 2007 issue of *Somerset Studio*. Her work has also appeared in the premiere issues of *Somerset Memories*, *Artful Blogger*, *Quilting Arts Gifts*, and *Life Images* and in *Fibre&Stitch* online magazine, as well as in *Somerset Wedding*, *Somerset Gallery*, *Somerset Home*, *Somerset Altered Couture*, and *Cloth Paper Scissors*. She has contributed to a number of artist's books, such as *1000 Artist Journal Pages* by Dawn Sokol, *True Vision* by L.K. Ludwig, and *The Creative Entrepreneur* by Lisa Sonora Beam. She also participates in various galleries and exhibits and conducts art workshops across the country and internationally.

A HAPPY LIFE.

These are the joys life gives to me,
Seeking for a fuller life;

Acknowledgments

AN ENORMOUS AMOUNT OF GRATITUDE goes to the entire team at Rockport/Quarry, especially my editor, Mary Ann Hall, for her kind, gracious spirit and expert guidance; my project manager, Betsy Gammons, for her wit and artistic counsel; and my copyeditor, Pat Price, for making sense of it all. Many thanks for making this dream a beautiful reality.

Very special thanks to my publisher, Winnie Prentiss, for giving me this opportunity to spread my wings.

My acknowledgments would not be complete without mentioning my sincere thankfulness for the unwavering love and support of my husband, Earl, who has always believed in me and in my pursuit of art. He has stood by me even in the most difficult moments of this journey and constantly urged me to never stop striving for my dreams. Thank you for being my knight in shining armor and for encouraging me to seek out my true passion. My love for you is now and forever without end.

A deep appreciation goes to my mother-in-law, Marylin Huskamp, for her steadfast friendship, wisdom, and wonderful sense of humor. I cherish all of our fun and crazy moments, as well as the quiet times.

Additional thanks go to my sister, Christa Nall, and brother-in-law, Brett Huskamp, for being my telephone lifelines across the miles. Your voices always make me smile.

And finally, I feel a great sense of honor to have been in the company of the many artists I have met and friends I have made along the way. You have added a richness to my being and a burning glow of memories that have woven themselves like threads into the days that make up this one, wonderful life!